YOU CAN'T CHEAT SUCCESS!

HOW THE LITTLE THINGS YOU THINK AREN'T IMPORTANT ARE THE MOST IMPORTANT OF ALL

TOM CORSON-KNOWLES

Copyright © 2013 by Tom Corson-Knowles

All Rights Reserved

No part of this publication may be reproduced, distributed, or transmitted in any form or by any means, including photocopying, recording, or other electronic or mechanical methods, or by any information storage and retrieval system without the prior written permission of the publisher, except in the case of very brief quotations embodied in critical reviews and certain other noncommercial uses permitted by copyright law.

Cambria and Calibri fonts used with permission from Microsoft.

Get the free Kindle publishing and marketing video training series here:

EbookPublishingSchool.com

Earnings Disclaimer

When addressing financial matters in any of our books, sites, videos, newsletters or other content, we've taken every effort to ensure we accurately represent our products and services and their ability to improve your life or grow your business. However, there is no guarantee that you will get any results or earn any money using any of our ideas, tools, strategies or recommendations, and we do not purport any "get rich schemes" in any of our content. Nothing in this book is a promise or guarantee of earnings. Your level of success in attaining similar results is dependent upon a number of factors including your skill, knowledge, ability, dedication, business savvy, network, and financial situation, to name a few. Because these factors differ according to individuals, we cannot and do not guarantee your success, income level, or ability to earn revenue. You alone are responsible for your actions and results in life and business. Any forward-looking statements outlined in this book or on our sites are simply our opinion and thus are not guarantees or promises for actual performance. It should be clear to you that by law we make no guarantees that you will achieve any results from our ideas or models presented in this book or on our sites, and we offer no professional legal, medical, psychological or financial advice.

Contents

WHY YOU SHOULD READ THIS BOOK	III
WHY I WROTE THIS BOOK	XIII
CHAPTER 1 A GUARANTEED PATH TO SUCCESS AND GREAT ACHIEVEMENTS	1
CHAPTER 2 DO THESE LITTLE THINGS BETTER AND YOUR SUCCESS IS ASSURED	19
CHAPTER 3 HOW TO THINK YOUR WAY TO SUCCESS	23
CHAPTER 4 A FEW SMALL HABITS THAT MAKE A BIG DIFFERENCE	29
CHAPTER 5 CREATING SUCCESS RIPPLES BY GIVING BACK	33
CONNECT WITH TOM	39
ABOUT THE AUTHOR	41
OTHER BOOKS BY TOM CORSON-KNOWLES	43
ONE LAST THING...	45
INDEX	47

WHY YOU SHOULD READ THIS BOOK

You can't cheat success! In any area of your life, regardless of what your goals or dreams are, you can't cheat success. Whether you want to retire early, start a successful business, have a great marriage, lose weight, travel the world, write a book, become a famous actress or actor, or anything else you feel is important to accomplish in your life, *you simply cannot cheat success.*

There are no shortcuts, magic bullets, or quick fixes. There is no magic genie who will grant you everything you want simply by asking. Contrary to the movie *The Secret,* you can't just sit on your couch visualizing a new car and have it manifest before your eyes without doing any work. If you want to achieve something truly great in your life, you must immediately stop looking for shortcuts. Stop taking the easy way out.

I know this probably isn't what you expected to read in a self-help book, but it's the message you need to hear. It's the message we all need to hear, and the lesson we should all be taught as young children. Success is earned through challenge. It's not something that comes easily and instantly.

So, if you can't cheat success, then how can you earn it legitimately? How can you achieve financial success, create incredible relationships, and live the life of your dreams?

First of all, you must discard your old habit of trying to cheat success. Get rid of your habits of limited thinking, limited action, and limitations in general. Understand that all worthwhile endeavors are challenging. Success comes from facing your challenges in life, not ignoring them.

Achieving success in life is an intellectual sport. You must think well in order to do well. The problem is that we're wired as human beings to make our decisions emotionally and not intellectually. How do we choose which job to take or where to live? For most of us, these major life choices are not carefully planned or strategized. Most of the time, we make important choices by simply going with the flow. If we grew up somewhere, we tend to stay there or, if we don't stay there, we tend to move wherever we have friends or family. Once we start on a path, we tend to continue on that route, never again questioning if we're doing the right thing or where we're headed.

The problem is this:

> *"If you don't have a carefully designed plan for your life, you'll simply follow the path of least resistance.*
>
> *And guess where that path is going? Nowhere!"*
>
> **TOM CORSON-KNOWLES**

The problem with following the path of least resistance is that it draws you in like the current of a mighty river. At first, you're excited at the progress you make as you swim downstream. However, eventually you realize that you don't really need to swim at all to keep moving. You can just float in the current, so you relax a little bit and let the current take you...

And then a year later, or five years later, or fifty years later, you look back at your life and realize you never really did follow your dreams. Sure, you saw those beautiful fields of opportunity, but you just floated on by instead of swimming against the current. You couldn't possibly be bothered to chase after your own dreams, could you? It's so much more comfortable just floating with the current instead!

After a while, you get knocked out of your stupor as you feel the current speed up and hear the sound of rapids ahead, but by then it's too late — you're caught in the flow and no matter how hard you try, you can't get out now. You end up tumbling over a waterfall. Your once comfortable life now seems like a nightmare.

This is exactly what happened to millions of Americans recently after the 2007-2008 Financial Crisis. Everyone was so comfortable buying big homes, charging up their credit cards, and going with the flow until the economic current changed. That kind of disaster is totally avoidable if you're using long-term thinking and avoiding emotional and psychological traps as we'll discuss in detail later in this book.

I'm sure some new age "thinkers" will argue with me on this point. They'll say, "Just go with the flow, man. There's no need to struggle. Life should be easy." That's ridiculous! Taking the easy path and going with the flow is exactly what causes most of human misery and suffering.

Most of us just go with the flow. A few brave souls, though, fought the current and dared to go after a dream. People like Steve Jobs, Gandhi, and Mother Theresa had the courage to fight for their dreams. They understood that life wasn't going to be easy fighting against the current. But it would definitely be worth the struggle.

Look at any part of nature and you will see that life is not easy at all. The only organisms on this planet that get lulled into a comfortable state of inaction are human beings. Every other form of life on this planet works their butts off to survive.

If you don't believe me, go out in nature and just start observing real life. Look at the ants that work around the clock collecting food. Watch what happens when ants come up to an obstacle in their perfectly crafted little ant path. Do the ants just sit down, grab a beer, and start watching TV when faced with a giant twig 1,000 times their size blocking their only known trail back to the ant colony? Of course not!

Those ants will go over, under, around, or through that tree. If it takes ten seconds or ten hours, those ants will do whatever it takes to get past that obstacle. *Ants will do whatever it takes to get past any obstacle!*

What do most people do when an obstacle comes up? One tiny obstacle, and we start to complain, cry or quit. I know that's how I used to treat most obstacles in life.

Us humans could learn a thing or two from ants. Instead of giving up when obstacles come, we must be willing to do whatever it takes to get past the obstacle and achieve our dreams in life.

Some might say, "But Tom, I've faced some really huge obstacles in my life! I couldn't possibly overcome them."

That's when I would mention that there are three kinds of people in this world: pessimists, optimists, and realists. Pessimists use negativity as an excuse not to do anything new or challenging. They say things like, "Yeah, I could start a business, but it wouldn't be successful. Have you seen the news about the economy?"

Pessimists love pessimistic friends and gossip media because it gives them other people to talk about all day instead of actually doing something. They see only the risk in every opportunity and, therefore, miss opportunities altogether. Pessimists have lost touch with reality, and they would rather talk about other people and events instead of struggling to overcome their obstacles in life.

But there's something even worse than a pessimist who has lost touch with reality. That would be an optimist with no sense of reality. The optimist who has lost touch with reality will start a business without any preparation or planning, tell all his friends he's about to get rich, invest all his savings and start the business with no plan, no mentors, and no guidance. Even worse, the optimist will do all this without any idea of what he's going to do when challenges come up. If you mention any risks to an optimist, they'll tell you "it's not a problem!" If an optimist invests in the stock market, he'll tell you there's no way it could ever crash.

Optimists see only opportunity and no risk. This is exactly what happened to millions of people who lost their homes in the 2007-2008 Financial Crisis. They were blinded by optimism and fell into numerous emotional and psychological traps from which many have still not recovered. Blind optimism is dangerous.

Now optimists can be wonderful people. They're certainly a lot more fun to be around than pessimists, but they're just as out of touch with the truth of life as pessimists. The key is to have a balance. The person who understands that balance is called a realist.

Realists see both opportunity and risk together. They're willing to look at both sides of the equation. They're willing to *think* about the world and see it for what it is. The greatest short history lesson of all time, according to Jim Rohn, is "opportunity mixed with difficulty." That's reality! If there are two things in life that are guaranteed, it's that you will have opportunities and you will have difficulties. There will always be a mix of both. Therefore, if you go into a situation in life where you only see difficulty or you only see opportunity, you ought to know immediately that you have a skewed view of reality. You can either correct your view, or face the consequences. Many bad decisions have been made because of an imbalanced perspective.

Instead of getting elated and optimistic or depressed and incredibly pessimistic, try to see both sides. Yes, you will get emotional when you think about anything truly important in your life. When you think about all the bad things that could happen you'll probably feel bad. When you think about all the wonderful things that could happen you'll probably feel good, but you must be willing to actually think honestly about the situation and not be emotionally attached to the opportunities or the risks.

For those of you who say life should be easy and you ought to just go with the flow, realize that is a single-minded way to look at the world. Life is both easy and hard. Life will give you rewards and punishments. You can't have one without the other. People who try to live a single-minded life end up stuck. That's taking the path of least resistance — that comfortable-looking path you ought to avoid.

HOW TO DESTROY 90% OF YOUR OBSTACLES IN LIFE IN 5 MINUTES

For those of you who say, "I can't achieve my dreams because of..." and then quickly follow that up with some kind of excuse, let me ask you this: *how good is your excuse?*

Were you born with no arms and no legs? Was life so painful knowing you were a burden to your family that you tried to drown yourself in a bathtub just to make their lives easier? Because that's what happened to Nick Vujicic, and he's now living his dream of inspiring people all around the world through his message of faith, love, and hope. Nick has influenced the lives of millions of people with more than 2,000 speeches in 44 countries. If you have two arms and two legs, what's your excuse?

Were you born into a dirt-poor family during a horrible war which threatened to destroy most of the world? Were you struck with an incurable, debilitating disease in your prime which left you in a wheelchair and told by the doctors that you wouldn't live more than two or three years? Were you at the bottom of your class in high school? Because that's what happened to Stephen Hawking, one of the most influential people in the field of physics and cosmology.

Were you torn away from your family and imprisoned in a concentration camp for years? Were your wife and family all murdered while you were sentenced to slave labor, living on moldy bread and unrecognizable porridge? That's what happened to Victor Frankl, who later wrote a best-selling book *Man's Search for Meaning*, and has forever left a legacy in the field of psychotherapy.

Were you repeatedly abused and raped as a child growing up? Did you grow up as a poor black woman trying to make it in a white man's world? These are just some of the challenges Oprah Winfrey had to deal with, and she's now a billionaire and one of the most influential people on the planet.

I could go on and on, but I think you get the point. If these people went through such horrible circumstances and went on to achieve such incredible feats in life, do you think it's possible that you could overcome whatever challenges you're facing and achieve something great as well? That's reality!

In fact, all four of these incredible people have said basically the same thing in one way or another, and I'll paraphrase it here for you:

> *"Even though this horrible thing happened to me, it actually made me stronger, and I'm now grateful for it because, by overcoming that obstacle, I become a stronger, better person."*

What if the challenges and struggles you are dealing with in life right now are actually good for you? What if they're helping you become a better, stronger person so that you can achieve your dreams? That's reality.

So if you want to conquer 90% of your obstacles in life right now, just think about all the people who have gone through so many challenging circumstances and still achieved great things in life. Then you'll realize you ought to be grateful for the amazing life and opportunities you do have. Then you'll realize that all those excuses and reasons why you can't be successful or achieve your dreams aren't real at all. And when you let go of those false limitations, at least 90% of the so-called obstacles in life will melt away. Will there be work left to do? Of course there will! But at least you'll be able to face your problems and challenges directly and appropriately without carrying around all that extra baggage.

ACTION STEPS

Grab your notebook or journal and a pen. Write down your three biggest problems or challenges right now. Then write down at least five reasons why you're grateful for that problem and how it's providing an opportunity for you to improve your life. If you can't think of any reasons to be grateful, use these questions as a guide:

- ? How is this situation serving me?
- ? What lessons could I learn here that could improve my life?
- ? How can I prevent a problem like this from happening in the future?
- ? If this is the biggest problem I have, how does it compare to the problems other people are facing right now?

- **?** Who is supporting me during this challenge? Can I be grateful for their support?
- **?** Is there someone who overcame a similar problem or challenge before? What can I learn from their experience?

WHY I WROTE THIS BOOK

Ever since I was a little child, I tried to cheat success. I remember not trying hard in school because it "wasn't worth it." I was a huge fan of the path of least resistance growing up. In fact, I would even argue with friends and anyone who would listen, telling them that taking the path of least resistance is ultimately the best path to take. Even after high school, I continued to take the easy way out much of the time.

I remember, when I was 19 years old, I started a part-time business in college selling a nutritional supplement. Why? Because I was scared of being stuck in an office job for the rest of my life. I wanted freedom — the ability to do what I wanted, whenever I wanted, wherever I wanted, and with whomever I wanted. Whether I was just trying to take a shortcut to success when I started the business, I don't know, but I started looking for shortcuts almost as soon I started!

I remember not making sales calls because it was uncomfortable and inconvenient. Honestly, I was just scared to pick up the phone and call people. I wouldn't follow up with every customer because some of them were "hard to get along with." I would take a week or two off from the business because I was "too busy." I had a list of excuses that would amaze you.

Eventually, I learned a big lesson the hard way. During my senior year in college, I was one of only 10 students selected for the #1 Best Entrepreneurship Course in America according to Inc.com.[1] It was called the Spine Sweat Experience. Here's how the course worked. It's spring semester of your final year in business school. You have to spend the entire semester creating a full business plan and then pitch your plan to a board of venture capitalists, angel investors, and wealthy entrepreneurs. If the investors like your business and want to invest in it, you get $4,000 in cash plus investors and mentors for your business, and you graduate. If the investors don't like your pitch, you fail the class, and can't graduate until the next semester.

Going into it, I was extremely optimistic. I thought it was going to be so easy because I wouldn't have to spend as much time in the classroom. It was the hardest semester of school in my life! When I pitched my business plan for a healthy quick service restaurant to the investors, the feedback they gave me was basically, "This is fantastic! Except you didn't put prices on the menu, so we're not interested."

I was furious. *"No prices on the menu… who cares?!"* I thought. I spent hundreds of hours of work researching, planning and practicing for that presentation. And the only thing that kept me from getting $4,000 in cash was the 15 minutes of work it would have taken to just write down prices on the menu. That was the most expensive 15 minutes of my life up to that point! Somehow I was allowed to pass the course, but I never did get the cash or an investment in the company.

That's when I started to understand that taking the path of least resistance doesn't pay. In fact, taking shortcuts is the most expensive thing you can do in life! It might look or feel easier to take a shortcut, but in the long run it's going to cost you far more than you can possibly imagine. And trust me, if you want to achieve anything great in life, it's more likely to be a long run that gets you there, not a shortcut. All great accomplishments take time. I'm not the only one

---

[1] http://www.inc.com/ss/best-entrepreneurship-courses-america#1

who has missed out on a big opportunity by simply neglecting one little detail. This kind of mistake happens every day.

Looking back on my life, I noticed that every reason I had for taking a shortcut was really just an excuse. I had great excuses for not trying hard in school, not making sales calls, and not putting prices on the menu in my business plan. That's why we take shortcuts — because we would rather create excuses for why we don't need to do something instead of doing what it takes to get what we really want. It's easier to make excuses than to get things done, but in the long run, that kind of behavior is incredibly counterproductive. We sabotage our own success by looking for a shortcut when what we should be doing is looking for the right thing to do.

Maybe that's why over 80% of businesses fail. The entrepreneurs who started them come up with some excuse as to why it won't work. Here are some typical excuses many business people make that keep them from achieving the success they truly desire:

- "The economy's bad."
- "The timing isn't right."
- "It's not my fault."
- "No one told me I had to do... (insert important activity here)."
- "I tried."

Even as I write these words right now, sitting at my computer, that little voice in my head is telling me, "It's okay, Tom... you don't have to try that hard. You don't have to write right now. You can go play in the pool and just relax..." And that's the voice that stops most people from achieving their dreams and goals in life.

What am I saying here? I'm saying you can either have excuses or you can have results. You can either let that little voice talk you out of doing great things with your life or you can ignore it and move on.

Let's move on, shall we?

Chapter 1

A Guaranteed Path to Success and Great Achievements

Even though there are no shortcuts in life, there are some things you can do to make your life a whole lot easier and more successful in the long run. The most powerful and life-changing thing you can do is to study.

In school, I was taught that studying is how you get good grades. But after school, there are no grades or report cards other than the ones you decide for yourself, like maybe your financial statement or how your family loves you. You get to decide what's important to you and what direction you want to go in life. If finances are important to you, then you ought to be studying financial statements, money management, investing, and so forth.

If having a wonderful marriage and family is important to you, you ought to be studying relationships, communication, marriage, and parenting. Otherwise, when challenges and obstacles come up, you'll be unprepared to deal with them.

"If you want to be successful, study success" said Jim Rohn. Read every book you can. Go to seminars, courses, and workshops. Find great mentors and teachers to guide you. Do whatever it takes to learn from and be around people who are where you want to be. That's what it means to study. The need for studying doesn't go away when you're finished with school. All humans must study in order to grow and achieve great things in life.

The amazing thing is that we now live in the "information age." We have more information available to us at any moment than we've ever had before in the history of the world. In a few seconds, any one of us could be studying anything we want. We could research a problem we have and find out how others have successfully solved that problem in just a few clicks on our smartphone or laptop.

Our society has basically compiled the largest problem-solving database in human history, accessible to anyone reading this book right now, and yet most of us only use this database to check Facebook or read the news instead of actually trying to figure out how to solve our own problems.

STUDY BEATS TALENT IN THE LONG RUN

I first learned about the power of studying when I was a senior in high school. I was recruited to the Quiz Bowl team by my English teacher and figured I'd try it out. It was a lot of fun for me, and I was made Captain of the team. I was the star player and scored a large number of points for the team by answering questions with random factoids about Greek mythology and definitions of uncommon words like diurnal.

At the time, I thought I was "the man." I was incredibly arrogant. I honestly believed I was the best Quiz Bowl player in the state. No team we faced ever had a player who could compete with me or answer nearly as many questions as I could. Because my teammates, coaches and friends told me I was good, and because I was usually winning, I deluded myself into thinking that I was the best because I had some talent for the sport.

But then one day I met my match. We went to a tournament in Indiana where several schools competed and the best teams would then face off for the tournament championship. We beat every team without much of a sweat and then we faced the other winning team for the championship from Brebeuf Jesuit Preparatory School. Five questions into the match, I knew there was something wrong. This teenager on the other team kept buzzing in and answering all the questions. He would buzz in before the questions were even finished and then answer them correctly. Half the time I wouldn't even know what the answer meant or how he even understood the question. These were obscure questions about ancient history and scientific phenomenon of which I had never even heard. I stared at him in awe. *I thought I was the best, but then I saw there was much more potential than I had previously imagined.*

The kid was a machine. He went on to score almost 200 points for his team, which in Quiz Bowl is an incredible feat. Most questions are worth 10 points, and games don't last that long so your opportunities for scoring are limited. We lost the game, and it was a brutal defeat. I was dumbfounded. *How could this guy be that smart? How could he possibly know the answers to all those questions?*

So I asked around later, and it turns out that *he actually studied for Quiz Bowl.* What a concept! Our team had practice once a week which lasted for about an hour and mostly involved joking around and answering a few questions for fun from trivia books or flash cards, but this kid actually studied every day for a few hours. He went through thousands of flash cards and trivia questions. He actually practiced with an intentional, deliberate, and well-thought out methodology for learning how to become a better Quiz Bowl player!

He didn't beat me because he was smarter than me (although he very well may have been), and he didn't beat me because he got lucky. He beat me because he studied to become a better quiz bowl player while I was busy playing video games. He made sacrifices to become a better player while I followed the path of least resistance. If we had a rematch 1,000 times, chances are he would have won every time. That's the power of studying—it almost guarantees your success when you learn how to do what you do better.

That's when I first started to realize that talent is insignificant. I have a talent for quiz bowl and trivia. I'm naturally curious and smart and have a good memory. But I will never, ever, ever be a *truly great* quiz bowl player because I am not willing to study trivial facts and information simply to become a better player. When it comes down to it, studying and practice will beat talent every time in the long run.

Of course, this is great news for those of us who aren't naturally gifted or don't seem to excel or shine in anything in particular. Personally, I know I'm not a very good writer, but I'm blessed to be earning a wonderful income from my books, and I continue to get better over time because I'm studying and practicing daily.

> *"If you want to achieve anything great in life, study and practice daily. If you just improve a little bit every day, before you know it, you will be one of the best in your field."*
>
> **TOM CORSON-KNOWLES**

If you've ever studied intensely in school or practiced piano or any other activity diligently, then you probably already understand how hard practicing actually is. It's not difficult to sit down at the piano for two hours and practice, but it's hard to focus your mind and concentrate on improving for two hours a day every day for the rest of your life. That's difficult. It takes a commitment. It's also the only way you're going to achieve greatness — through diligent, regular practice.

HOW TO KILL MEDIOCRITY ONCE AND FOR ALL AND ACHIEVE GREATNESS

Here's a simple exercise to help you kill mediocrity once and for all and achieve greatness in life.

STEP 1: AIMING FOR GREATNESS

First, grab your notebook or journal and a pen.

Now write down what you would love to do with your life. Answer the following questions:

- **?** What would you like to achieve?
- **?** If you could do anything, if there were no limitations, what would you like to do with your life?
- **?** If your life could leave a legacy for the world, what would it be?
- **?** If you could make the world a better place, how would you do it?
- **?** *If you had a magic wand and you could use it to change the world, how would you change it?* (Chances are you don't need a magic wand to change the world; you just need the courage to start taking action to make that change).

Now that you've answered these questions in your journal and spent some time thinking about what you really want to do with your life, it's time to take your list of goals and dreams and reality test them.

STEP 2: REALITY TESTING FOR GREATNESS

Now that you've got some dreams and goals written down, some things that you're excited about accomplishing if you only knew how, it's time to reality test them. This is not the kind of reality test normal people do on an everyday basis. When I first told my friends that I was going to start a business in college and work from home instead of getting a job in an office or cubicle, they all laughed at me. They said I wasn't being "realistic" and that it would never work. Well, three years later they were all looking for jobs, and I was traveling the world with the income from my home-based business.

Obviously, they weren't being realistic about my dreams, and that's the case with most of us. When it really comes down to it, most of us are doubters. Most of us have a mean pessimistic streak running through us and when someone says something that's outside of our comfort zone, our warning lights go off and we think "that's not realistic!"

So the first thing you want to do when reality testing your dreams is to look at the dreams you have and honestly assess them by yourself. Don't tell your friends, family, or anyone else about your dreams when you're first starting out. Keep them to yourself until you've already committed to them and have a plan of action in place. Otherwise, you'll just get a bunch of people who don't know what they're talking about trying to tell you that you can't do what it is you want to do with your life.

Here's how you can honestly and realistically assess your dreams and goals. Write down the following questions and answer them:

HAS ANY HUMAN BEING IN HISTORY EVER ACHIEVED THIS?

If there's anyone in the history of the world who has achieved what you've set out to achieve, then obviously it's realistic. The goal I set for myself years ago of earning a full-time income working from home has been achieved by millions of people in probably every country in the world. It's clearly a realistic goal. Now, that doesn't mean that everyone in the world who *wants* that goal has achieved it. It just means that others have done it. If anyone else has ever done it, then it is *definitely* possible for you.

In helping hundreds of people set and achieve goals throughout my life in business, I've noticed that almost every goal or dream people have falls into this category. Almost everything people want has already been achieved before by someone else. If you want a million dollar net worth, you can find millions of people who have already achieved that. If you want a wonderful marriage with two kids, you can find millions of people who have already achieved that.

If your dreams and goals have been accomplished by someone else before, here's all you have to do to achieve them:

1. Commit to studying and practicing as much as you possibly can to achieve your goal.

2. Find people who have already accomplished what you want to accomplish and *invest as much of your time as possible being with and learning from these people.* By spending time with people who have achieved what you want to achieve, you'll realize that they're just like you. They weren't given some special or unique talent that made them successful. They just have different habits and do things a little differently. You can learn from them how to

do things differently so that you can get the same kind of results! **NOTE:** Be careful who you study from and what you attempt to learn from them. It would be foolish to try to learn relationship skills from your wealthy friend who has poor relationships. Study wealth from such a friend, but be careful not to pick up their relationship habits.

3. Never give up. When things get tough, when you feel like quitting, when it's not working out... just realize that if someone else can do it, you can do it. But you'll never achieve your goal if you quit.

Now, if you have a dream or a goal that no human being has ever accomplished before, than that's truly something special, and it's going to require a little something extra.

Doing Something Totally New

If you're one of the rare people who have a goal or dream to achieve something totally new that's never been done before, then you are a very special person indeed! Few people ever set such goals or dream of such unique dreams. Most of us just want what others have already achieved. Most of us want a nice home with a happy family, enough money that we don't have to worry about finances, and to make a difference in our community by helping those less fortunate, and so forth. These are average dreams and goals, and they're quite common.

There's nothing wrong with average dreams and goals. But if everything you wrote down before is average and has already been achieved by someone else, then I would just encourage you to dig a little deeper. What do you *really* want in life? If you could accomplish *anything*, what would you really do? Let go of any perceived limitations and then dream from there. What would be possible for your life if there were nothing holding you back?

If you believe in God or a Creator or even just evolution, than you know that every single human being on this planet is unique. Every one of us is special in our very own ways. And if every one of us is special and unique, why should our dreams and goals be the same as everyone else's? Every truly great person I've ever met has a dream or a goal to do something truly unique.

If you ask the question, "Has any human being in history ever achieved this?" and the answer truly is "no", you've got something special there. Now, how can we honestly assess whether or not that dream or goal is realistic?

Write down and answer this question to help you get more clarity:

IS THIS GOAL OR DREAM JUST A DIFFERENT, BETTER, OR IMPROVED VERSION OF SOMETHING THAT HAS ALREADY BEEN ACCOMPLISHED BEFORE BY SOMEONE ELSE?

For example, if you have a goal to save polar bears from extinction or create a net worth of $100 billion or create a device that creates unlimited free energy, those are all entirely "new."

No one has ever saved polar bears from extinction, had a net worth of $100 billion, or created a free energy device as of 2014. But there are people who have made progress in those areas or come close to achieving those goals.

There are people who have come close. There are scientists who have put a lot of time and energy into studying polar bears and creating a way to save them from extinction. There are even people who have saved other species of animals from extinction and you could probably learn from their success in a similar but different arena.

Warren Buffett has a net worth of around $60 billion. It's not quite $100 billion, but it's close. If achieving great wealth is your dream, study and learn from wealthy people. There are people who have been studying fusion and other technologies to create a free energy device as well. You could study and learn from them.

So, even though these goals may seem unrealistic because no one has ever achieved them before, and they may seem impossible to most people, they're really not unrealistic at all. It's pretty easy to see that if Warren Buffet just invested his money wisely for a few more years, he could probably have a $100 billion net worth. And if scientists study a little more, it's easy to imagine that there might be some solution that could save polar bears from extinction. And it's easy to imagine that some scientist may yet discover a way to use fusion or some other technology to create a free energy device. It may not be *likely* that these things will happen, but it's definitely *possible*.

Even these outlandish goals which may seem ridiculous and impossible at first are actually quite possible when you think about it, so I can guarantee you that whatever your dreams or goals are, they are realistic. It's possible, to say the least. And as long as it's possible, you can achieve what you set out to accomplish if you're willing to do whatever it takes to achieve your goals and dreams.

In my limited personal experience, every goal or dream someone creates has either already been achieved before or someone else has already made progress in that area. There are very few truly unrealistic dreams and often they come about because of people trying to change the way the universe works, which we'll discuss shortly.

REALISTIC GOALS VS. REALISTIC PLANS

It's one thing to have a realistic goal, but it's an entirely different thing to have a realistic plan. Most of us have realistic goals. Very few people have realistic plans to achieve those goals. That's where most people fail.

Let's talk about money for a moment because it's easy to count and measure progress along the way toward a financial goal. I'm going to show you how to apply this process to achieve a financial goal, but realize that this same process will work with any goal and in any area of life.

STEP 1. CLARIFY YOUR GOAL WITH SUPER SPECIFICITY

First you must clarify your goal. Be as specific as you possibly can. For example, instead of setting a financial goal to get rich and retire early, set a very clear and specific goal to earn $10 million by January 1, 2018, for example.

Unclear goal: I want to get rich and retire early.

Clear goal: I want to have a net worth of $10 million on January 1, 2018.

"What's the difference?" you might say. The difference is astronomical!

Here's an example of how setting specific goals can make a huge difference in the results you will achieve...

Because of my published books and educational videos and courses on writing, publishing, and marketing books, I get emails on a daily basis from authors looking for help, advice, and ideas. And I'm happy to help! But I'm able to help some much more than others—and the main reason is because of clarity.

Here's an example of two requests I've received via email recently:

> **Email request #1:** "My books aren't selling well. I really want to sell more books, but I'm not sure how. I've tried blogging and social media but nothing's working. Any ideas?"
>
> **Email Request #2:** "I have a blog where I write about nutrition and fitness, and I would love to use the blog to sell more books. Can you please take a look at my blog (link) and let me know one or two things I can do right now to sell more books?"

Guess which person I was able to help more? The author who sent email #2. It took me two minutes to look at her blog and, I gave her three solid ideas for how she could sell more books on her site. Reading the email, looking at her site, and writing the reply took less than 3 minutes total, and I was happy to help.

Then there's email #1... I spent 10 minutes trying to respond to this email. I really wasn't sure what to say or how to say it. The question is so broad that it actually confused me. I thought, *"Should I tell her about how to create a great title, book cover, write a hot book description, do keyword research, advanced SEO strategies, publicity, guerrilla marketing, social media, connecting with bloggers, forum marketing, or something else?"* Because the question was so broad, it opened up the entire universe of possibilities, which can be far too much when you want to solve a specific problem. I already invested thousands of hours in research and writing on how to sell more books. I thought, *"Should I just write an essay that summarizes all the essential pieces to marketing books?"* but then I decided that would take hours to write, and I've already done so in my books. I won't bore you with the details, but it took me far longer to reply to the first email than the second. Why? Because it wasn't clear at all! I didn't know what books the person had published, where they were published, what the titles were, what the covers looked like, or anything else. I knew next to nothing about this person and here I am supposed to give them the secret to success in an email?

Why was it so hard to help one person and yet so incredibly easy to help the other? Because when you're clear on what you want, it's easy to find what you need to get it. When you're unclear about what you want, it's almost impossible to find what you need to get it.

Here's the deal: If you're not absolutely clear about what you want, you're never going to get it until you get clear! And if you can't clearly articulate the problem you have that you're trying to solve, no one else can help you solve it.

Someone once told me that a confused mind always says no. And it's true! Whenever you find yourself confused or unclear, chances are you will just give up. We need a clear vision, a clear goal to move toward in order to do something, especially something challenging. *Let specificity become your friend and never again hang out with vagueness or generality.*

When you begin to set clear goals and clear objectives to achieve your dreams with a clear plan of action, you'll find it much easier to find the resources, people, and connections you need to succeed. But until you get clear, you'll feel like a man with a blindfold trying to find his way through a maze. It's a lot easier to find your way in life without a blindfold. And the only way to take that blindfold off is to get clear about what you want and where you're going.

Now that you're clear about your goal and have specified what you want, it's time to figure out where you are right now.

STEP 2. DETERMINE YOUR EXACT STARTING POINT

The first place to start when you're creating a plan to achieve your goals and dreams is to figure out *where are you now?*

Write down in your notebook: where am I now on the path to achieving this goal?

Let's say your goal is to retire in 5 years so that you can spend more time with your family and do whatever you enjoy doing instead of working.

The first thing you're going to do is write down where you are now. Write down your age, your net worth, and your current income, and expenses per month.

Then write down the exact numbers for your age, net worth, income, and expenses as you want them to be when your goal is achieved.

Be honest with yourself here. If you have to look up the numbers, invest the time to look up the numbers. Don't try to take shortcuts here. The more precise you are, the faster you will achieve your goals, because better information leads to better decisions.

STEP 3. CALCULATE THE DIFFERENCE OR GAP

Now that you know your exact goal and your exact starting point, it's time to calculate the difference. For money, this is a simple exercise. Simply subtract your current net worth, income, and expenses from your goal numbers and that's your difference.

For more intangible goals, it might be a bit more difficult to calculate a difference. Let's say your goal is to create an incredible marriage. Well, what's the difference between that outcome and where you are now? You could imagine a scale of 1 to 10 with 10 being your ultimate goal in this area. Where do you see yourself now? Then you can roughly calculate the difference.

It's incredibly important that you be as detailed and accurate with your calculations as possible. Don't try to "fudge" the numbers. Don't try to make yourself look better than you are. Be completely honest with yourself. If you can't even be honest with yourself, how can you be honest with anyone else?

Without complete honesty and authenticity about where you are, you'll find it incredibly difficult to get where you want to go. Without honesty, you won't truly be able to see what *really* needs to be done for you to improve. Honesty is always the best policy.

STEP 4. CREATE A PLAN TO MAKE PROGRESS

Notice that I wrote to create a plan to *make progress*. Not a plan to *get there*. The reason this is so important is that with many goals you may not have *any idea how you can get there*. But you'll know how you can make progress!

> For example, if you're earning $30,000 a year right now and you have a goal to earn a million dollars a year, you might not have any idea how you're going to get there! But I'm sure you have many ideas for how you can make progress and approach your goal.
>
> There's nothing wrong with setting a goal to earn a million dollars a year if you only earn $30,000 a year, but if you pretend that you know exactly how to get there when you have no clue, that's just fooling yourself.

Many people have gone from modest incomes to earning incredible fortunes, but no one got there overnight. It takes steady progress over time. All you have to concern yourself with right now is getting started and making progress!

Here's how:

- ➢ Grab a notebook with paper and pen and write down these questions and answer them for yourself:
- ➢ What can I do today to increase my income?
- ➢ What can I do to increase my savings?
- ➢ What can I do to get around people who have already achieved this goal?

The answers to these questions will lead you in the right direction. Chances are you already know how to earn more money, but you're not doing it. You might have some old items lying around in the garage. Could you sell them on eBay or Amazon to earn some extra cash? Then you can save that cash and increase your net worth.

Can you provide a service for your community? If you make $500 selling old stuff you didn't even want any more on eBay, maybe you could help your neighbors sell stuff online and have them pay you a percentage of how much you help them earn. That's a real win-win. I know teenagers who have used this exact strategy to earn thousands of dollars, and I even know one young man who used this exact strategy to earn over a million dollars before he was 18.

Now I'm not saying that selling stuff on eBay is the key to getting rich. It's just one simple idea that many people have already used to earn more money. You probably have even better ideas for how you can earn more money. Write down your own ideas and put them into action.

After you've written down the answers and chosen a path, take action *right now!* If you have an idea to earn more money, take one step right now toward that goal. If you need to make a phone call, go make it. If you need to do some research online, get started. Don't sit around hoping your dreams will come true. You've got to get off your butt and get started. Strike while the idea is fresh in your mind and your motivation is at its strongest point.

Now that you've learned how to set realistic goals and create a clear plan to make progress, let's talk about unrealistic goals and dreams.

UNREALISTIC GOALS AND DREAMS

Now there *are* some totally unrealistic goals and dreams. They're few and far between, but they're actually far more common than you might think by now. Here are some of the most common unrealistic goals and dreams people cling to:

"I want to get rich without working."

"I want to be happy all the time."

"I never want to get hurt again."

"I want life to be easy."

"I want to lose weight without changing my diet or lifestyle."

You'll notice most of these unrealistic goals have a common theme. Most people either want something for nothing. You can't achieve something without paying the price of success.

Wanting to get rich without working is a common delusion where someone wants something for nothing. "For every action there is an equal and opposite reaction" is a law. Newton stated it this way:

> *"To every action there is always an equal and opposite reaction: or the forces of two bodies on each other are always equal and are directed in opposite directions."*

You can actually visualize how this law works and see clearly how to apply it for the rest of your life. Visualize yourself standing in a room with nothing but a ball hanging on a chain that's roughly your height. Let's imagine that getting the ball to come to you is your goal. Trying to get that ball to come to you without you doing anything is impossible. It will just stay there. But if you push the ball away from you, it will swing back. That's Newton's law in action. In order to *get* something you must *give* something. Everything in the universe is balanced.

That brings us to the other common unrealistic types of goals: one-sided goals. This happens when we want only one part of life without the equal and opposite part of life. Say you want to be happy and never sad. Or say you want to feel joy but never hurt. These are impossible wants. The universe is balanced. We must live with both sides. Wanting to change the fabric of the universe itself is futile and unrealistic.

Learn to take the good with the bad. Take the joy with the hurt. Take the happy with the sad. How would you know what real happiness is without sadness? There would be nothing to compare it to. It would just be normal. And boring. And incredibly unrealistic.

If you find yourself with unrealistic goals or dreams, reframe it. Instead of trying to just experience one side of life, embrace both sides. Here's how:

EMBRACING THE BALANCE OF LIFE

Grab your notebook and pen. Write down and answer these questions:

HOW DOES THIS (NEGATIVE SIDE) BENEFIT ME?

For example, if your goal is to "never be hurt again," then go back to a recent experience where you felt hurt and ask yourself *how did this experience benefit me?*

WHAT DID YOU LEARN FROM BEING HURT? WHAT BENEFITS DID YOU RECEIVE THAT YOU MIGHT NOT BE APPRECIATING RIGHT NOW?

Here's an example from my own life...

When I was thirteen years old, I started dating my first girlfriend with whom I was absolutely infatuated. I thought she was just amazing. She was gorgeous. I thought I had died and gone to Heaven when we started dating. She was my first kiss. One day, I called her and her mom answered the phone with a gruff voice. I was confused why her mom seemed so angry. Then my girlfriend picked up the phone and immediately started yelling at me. She said "I don't want to be with you anymore!" and then hung up. I was crushed. I had no idea why she dumped me.

I kept thinking over and over... *Did I do something wrong? Why was she being so mean? What happened? I thought we were in love?* I was heartbroken for months. Being hurt feels horrible. I still held a grudge against her until many years later when I learned this simple exercise.

I grabbed a notebook and wrote down this question:

HOW DID THIS EXPERIENCE BENEFIT ME?

At first, I couldn't imagine any benefits. I saw only the negatives. I saw the hurt she had caused me. I saw the embarrassment with my friends when I had to tell them she dumped me. I felt the anger and sadness she caused me. I saw no benefits. However, I knew that every experience in life has positive and negative aspects, and I was determined to let this long-held resentment go, so I kept thinking... *How did this experience benefit me?*

Well, she did teach me how to kiss. I guess that's a plus. It was really embarrassing not having kissed anyone before, but she taught me and that skill definitely came in handy in later relationships, so that's a pretty big plus.

Then, I thought it did feel really good to care about someone so much. Whether it was love or infatuation, it just felt good to love someone that way even if it didn't last, so she taught me how to love someone else to some extent. That's pretty important!

Then, I thought that she did teach me an important lesson: beauty is only skin deep. Just because a woman or a man is beautiful or handsome on the outside doesn't mean she or he is worth spending time with. I learned that I needed to have enough respect for myself to not spend too much time with people who weren't kind to me. Another big lesson!

On and on, I kept writing down all the benefits of that experience. It was amazing! I had a list of over 21 ways that relationship benefitted me. All the experiences I had, the lessons I learned, and the new relationships I created were valuable for me. By the time I was done writing, I was so inspired I had tears in my eyes and love in my heart. All that anger, sadness, and resentment was gone forever. I don't carry those horrible attachments with me anymore. I've embraced the balance of negative and positive in my life.

Have you?

Invest the time in doing this exercise. Choose a difficult or challenging experience in your past that still makes you feel angry, sad, hurt or another painful emotion.

Then write down this question in your notebook or journal:

How did this experience benefit me?

Write down as many lessons and positive benefits you received from that experience as possible. Don't stop until the negative emotions and pain are gone or greatly diminished. When you start to become grateful for that painful experience, you'll know you're making progress. This is how you let go of emotional baggage so that you can move forward with less struggle and pain.

Chapter 2
Do These Little Things Better and Your Success Is Assured

The opposite of trying to take shortcuts to success is proactively looking for ways you can do more, serve more, and make a bigger difference in the world. Napoleon Hill calls this the habit of going the extra mile.

Going the extra mile is what makes the difference between those who succeed and those who do 99% of the work and yet still fail like I did in my entrepreneurship class. It's that extra 1% that makes all the difference — and the truth is, it's not much extra work at all! They key is to simply develop the habit of going the extra mile.

I was traveling in Bangkok recently and a friend recommended I stop by a certain tailor in the city who creates exceptional tailored suits and dress shirts. I decided to walk four blocks to the tailor from my hotel, and I noticed at least 7 different tailors along the way with fine silk ties, incredible suits, and very nice dress shirts. I also noticed that every single tailor I walked past was empty — there was not one customer inside any of those shops while I strolled past.

Then I finally found what I was looking for — a little sign that said "Rajawongse," so I walked in, and I was amazed to find the place was packed. There were at least 6 other customers in the store, and I had to wait in line just to talk to the tailor! I was immediately offered refreshments — free beer, wine, liquor, water, tea, whatever I wanted. Then I was told I could pick out some colors I liked and I could talk to the tailor afterwards.

As I walked around the store, I noticed some very curious details. First, there was a news clipping about the owners of the store, Jesse and Victor, and how they landed President Bush senior as a client and later his son. President Obama was also a client. The owners had a client list so full of dignitaries, law enforcement professionals, and federal agents, I found myself wondering if the Secret Service might walk into the store any moment.

I also noticed the suits were all made of the finest Italian Merino wool. Later, I overheard Jesse saying on the phone to another customer that they buy all their material directly from the supplier so that the customers can get the best price. Needless to say, I walked out with the finest tailored suit made from the finest Italian Merino wool from a tailor who's worked with multiple United States Presidents, and I paid less than I did for a cheap suit I bought from a mall in Indiana.

Jesse and Victor definitely understand the habit of going the extra mile. From the way they treat customers, to the quality of the materials, to their craftsmanship, to delivery, and follow-up, they're true masters at doing little things extraordinarily well. Needless to say, I've referred more than a few people to this little tailor shop in Bangkok called Rajawongse.

But that's not all! When I was about to leave the shop, the owner asked if I needed any investors for my business. He said he'd be happy to introduce me to any investors if I needed it. Now I don't know if you've ever owned a business, but I can tell you this: in my 7 years of owning a business, I have never once had anyone I was purchasing a product from ask me if I needed investors or offer to introduce me to potential business partners. That's kind of like if you're unemployed and you buy a suit from someone and then they ask you if you need a job because they happen to have a few hundred friends that are hiring right now and will give you all the money you want. It's one of the kindest, most generous and thoughtful gifts someone could give you — and it didn't cost him a dime.

I can tell you this much — I will never buy a suit from anyone else for the rest of my life. Why would I even want to buy a suit from anyone else? I get a great suit at a great price and get to do business with great people who care about me and want to help me.

When you go the extra mile, the people you live with, work with, and hang out with will always be glad to have you around because you will set yourself apart with your willingness to help and serve others. They will be loyal to you because they know you want the best for the. When you go out of your way to help people, you set yourself apart from the masses that are just going with the flow.

No matter what you want to achieve in life, you'll need other people to help you get there. And nothing will attract people to you faster than going the extra mile and helping others in ways that no one else does. And it doesn't cost much. It's free to ask someone if they need an introduction to someone who can help them. It's free to go out of your way to be kind to someone or to remember their birthday. Most of the truly valuable things in life are completely free and most people ignore them because there is no price tag.

If you can add enough value to other people's lives, you can achieve anything you want in your life.

Action Steps

Grab your journal and pen and write down and answer these questions:

- **?** How can I add more value to my family?
- **?** How can I add more value to my community?
- **?** How can I add more value to society?
- **?** How can I add more value to my friends?
- **?** How can I add more value to the people I interact with on a daily basis?
- **?** How can I add more value to the world?
- **?** How can I add more value to the universe?

? Can I do this better than anyone else in the world? Can I do it with more kindness, love, fun, humor, creativity, or something else?

The more value you add to the world, the better the world and your life will be.

CHAPTER 3
HOW TO THINK YOUR WAY TO SUCCESS

We talked briefly earlier about clear thinking, but I want to dive even more deeply into this incredibly important activity that is commonly ignored.

Clear thinking is a key to success, and it requires going the extra mile. It requires not taking shortcuts or looking for an easy way out. It requires sitting down and seriously *thinking* until you get clear.

Albert Einstein said:

> *"We cannot solve our problems with the same thinking we used when we created them."*

Now I know that quote has been thrown around almost everywhere, but few people actually know how to think *differently*.

Think about it this way: how do most of your problems come about? How are you thinking when you create most problems?

I don't know about you, but most of my problems come about when I'm unconsciously thinking. It's when I'm just going through the motions and not thinking about what I'm doing — that's when mistakes happen and problems are created. The vast majority of our problems are caused by old habits performed unconsciously.

If unconscious thinking is what causes most of our problems in the first place than doesn't it make sense that *conscious* thinking might help us come up with better solutions?

It still amazes me that in all my years of school from pre-school to business school, I never once had a teacher who taught me how to think (it's quite possible they did try to teach me but I just wasn't ready to learn at the time).

I had to go out of my way to study and learn from successful people, and eventually I learned a little thinking exercise that changed my life. Now I'm going to share it with you.

THE CONSCIOUS THINKING PROCESS

Conscious thinking is a process that requires you to actively ponder questions. The better questions you ask yourself, the better your answers will be. The better your answers, the better options you'll have. And the better options you have, the better choices you will make. And, of course, the better choices you make, the better your life will be and the more success you will experience in your life.

So, all great thinking starts with great questions.

Let's begin the Conscious Thinking Process.

STEP 1. ASK GREAT QUESTIONS

I keep a list of great questions in my journal at all times. Whenever I have a problem, I ask myself questions from my list and, without fail, I always feel better after thinking.

Here are some examples of questions I've found to be incredibly useful for solving problems and creating more success in my life:

? What can I do today to improve my relationships?

? What can I do today to improve my health?

- ? What can I do today to improve my self-esteem?
- ? What can I learn that will help improve my life?
- ? What can I do today to earn more money?
- ? How can I help and serve more people?
- ? Has anyone ever solved this problem before? If so, how can I learn from them how to solve this problem more effectively?
- ? How did I create this problem in the first place? Is there anything I can do in the future to prevent similar problems from occurring?
- ? Is there anything I should stop doing that would improve my life?

STEP 2. ANSWER THESE QUESTIONS RIGHT NOW!

After you write down and ask yourself these questions, answer them! You have all the answers inside you — the problem is that you haven't been asking the right questions. This is where conscious thinking gets its power because it forces you to answer the questions that will get you the information and ideas you need to solve your problems and move forward.

Chances are, you already know deep down inside you everything you need to know to solve your problems and achieve your dreams.

This process will help you rediscover this knowledge inside you and then put it into action.

STEP 3. TAKE ACTION RIGHT AWAY

Once you've answered your questions and found new ideas, solutions, and tools to help solve your problems, it's time to take action. If you need to consult with someone who's solved your problem before, reach out to them and contact them. If you've already come up with a possible solution, go ahead and start implementing it.

It's not good enough to just think of a great idea — you have to put it into action!

STEP 4. DEBRIEF AND REPEAT

Once you've implemented your new ideas and action steps, it's time to debrief and review your results. Did things go as planned? If not, what new problems or situations came up? How can you solve those new problems? What can you learn from what went well and what didn't go well?

The power of conscious thinking is that it forces you to quickly identify and solve your problems rather than ignoring them or pretending like they're not important. Trust me, there's a huge difference between five years of experience in life and five years of experience solving problems and making progress in business. Far too many people have years of experience but they ignored many of their problems instead of solving them!

If you truly want more success in your life, nothing will get you there faster than using conscious thinking to consistently solve your problems quickly.

You don't need a guru or someone else to tell you what to do. Can others help point you in the right direction? Absolutely! But you can be your own guide as well when you practice conscious thinking. When you combine your own inner guidance with the guidance of great teachers and mentors, you will solve more problems and achieve your goals and dreams much faster.

YOUR PROBLEMS WILL NEVER GO AWAY

At this point, I feel I need to warn you that even though you will become an incredibly effective problem solver when you begin using conscious thinking, you will always have problems. As soon as you solve one problem, another will replace it. This is actually a wonderful thing!

Every time you solve a new problem, another will takes its place. This is called progress. If you own a business and have a problem of not having enough customers, as soon as you solve that problem and get plenty of customers, you will have dozens of more problems to deal with! You'll probably have to work more or hire more help. You'll probably have to improve your customer service systems and delivery, and much, much more. These are great problems to have! These are growth problems.

The worst situation is to have the same problems over and over again and never learn to solve them. That's the life of someone with just five years of experience. They've got five years of experience with the same problems. Trust me, if you have the same problems five years from now that you do today, you'll be in a miserable state of mediocrity and stagnation. You'll end up feeling like your life isn't going anywhere.

As you consistently solve your problems and create new ones, you'll be growing personally and professionally. You'll become a better, stronger, wiser, and more capable person. But you'll still have problems. And you can tell the size of the person by understanding the size of their problems.

One person's problem is how to afford her rent so that she can live in a home. Another person's problem is how to pay the mortgage on his 1,000 unit apartment so that 1,000 families can live in a home. Another person's problem is how to design an entire city so that millions of people can have homes. Another person's problem is how to design a country so that the entire country can have homes. And a few individuals think even bigger. Their problem is how to design the world so that all people can have a home. And a very few people think even bigger. Their problem is how to design the world so that all creatures can have a home.

Can you see how a little change of perspective can make a huge difference in what you can accomplish in life?

The bigger the problems you solve, the bigger the impact you will have in the world. One of the basic human needs we all have is contribution. We all want to feel like our life makes a difference. And I can tell you from personal experience and from studying thousands of incredibly successful, wise, and accomplished people that the bigger the problems you go for in life, the more you will feel like your life makes a difference. And that, to me, is the greatest success of all.

Chapter 4

A Few Small Habits That Make a Big Difference

Do the Best You Can, Especially on Little Things

There are no little things in life! Everything matters. T. Harv Eker says:

> *"The way you do anything is the way you do everything."*

If you try to cut corners and take shortcuts in your job, I guarantee you're doing it in other areas of your life. Take a look at *how* you do what you do. Do you find yourself whining, complaining, making excuses or giving up in one area of your life? If you do, and you start to pay attention, you'll notice yourself making those same mistakes in just about every area of your life. That's the bad news.

But there's good news, too. If you can eliminate these bad habits in one area of your life, chances are those results will transfer over to just about every area of your life. That's why there are no small things in life. When you make a little change in one area of life, it can end up making a huge difference in other areas of your life.

Don't let little things slide. Learn to master the little things in life, and the big problems will become a lot easier to master.

BE WILLING TO DO WHAT'S UNCOMFORTABLE OR DIFFICULT

Do you feel uncomfortable or scared to make a change in your life that you think would be good for you? If so, that means it's probably one of the best things you could do for your life.

When you do what's uncomfortable, scary and difficult, you grow. When you grow, you become better. When you become better, you achieve more. When you achieve more, you get closer to your goals and dreams.

All that progress starts by doing something difficult. Don't run away from challenges. Run toward them. That's the most direct path to success, but it's not a shortcut.

STOP LOOKING FOR SHORTCUTS

Instead of looking for a shortcut or an easier way, begin to look for challenges.

Instead of looking at your strengths, look at your weak spots.

Instead of blaming those you work with, look for better coaches, mentors and teachers.

Instead of failing because you don't know how to succeed, look for new ideas, knowledge and education.

Instead of working just to get money or complete a task, look for opportunities to grow, expand, and improve in your work.

CREATE THE HABIT OF FINISHING WHAT YOU START NO MATTER HOW TOUGH THINGS GET

Imagine how much you would have accomplished in your life if you had never given up. Sometimes our goals and dreams change, and we quit because the activity is no longer best for us. But more often, we quit because things get tough. If you can persevere until you finish, you'll begin to achieve goals and dreams that you never thought were possible..

START SMALL

Be willing to do things very poorly at first so that you can practice and learn to do them very well over time. Anything worth doing is worth doing poorly at first. Don't focus on your lack of skills. Focus on making progress. As long as you're making progress and doing the best you can, you can't fail. Failure is quitting. Failure isn't making a mistake. Everyone makes mistakes. It's what you do after your mistakes that determines your success.

BECOME A BETTER PERSON

Results are just the outcome naturally flowing from the person you've become. When you work on something that challenges you, you will become a better person.

Don't try to fit in by being normal or average. Strive to be the best you can be, whatever that means for you. Don't put arbitrary limits on yourself based on what you think you can do or based on what others have done.

VISUALIZE YOUR SUCCESS

Here's another powerful exercise for you.

Visualize yourself right now as someone facing your current worst nightmares and challenges. Now multiply those fears and challenges by ten. See yourself facing those challenges without whining, without excuses, without looking for shortcuts, without waiting for the perfect timing. See yourself full of courage, being proactive, and taking action. See yourself overcoming those challenges. Now feel how good it feels to have achieved your goals even in spite of these obstacles which are far worse than anything you've ever faced before.

Imagine how successful you would be with no excuses, no whining, no looking for shortcuts, and no waiting for the perfect time to get started.

Chapter 5

Creating Success Ripples by Giving Back

Solving huge problems isn't the only way to feel like your life makes a difference and to make a contribution in the world. Sometimes small things can make a big difference.

No matter where you are in your life or how successful you are right now, you have the opportunity to give back and make a huge difference in other people's lives. One huge benefit of becoming a great problem solver in your own life is that you can use those skills to help solve important problems for others. It's the ultimate form of giving back.

Giving back to others isn't just a great thing to do *after* you've become successful. It's a great thing to do to help you become more successful! The more you give to others, the more you will receive in return. In this chapter, we're going to discuss some important ways you can give back to others, and in the process take you to an even higher level of success.

Let's discuss the five key ways you can give back.

SERVICE WORK

Service work is the work of great people like Mother Theresa. There are millions of wonderful people all over the world who serve others without asking for anything in return. These are the giant, humble people who make the world a better place, often without any recognition.

You can do great service work by volunteering at a local homeless shelter, cleaning up trash in your community, and in a myriad of other ways. Service work is when you donate your time, love, and energy to help others. It's a wonderful way to give back and make a difference in the world.

FINANCIAL CHARITY

Financial charity is another great way to give back. This is when you donate your money to an organization or cause that helps and serves others. Financial charity is what pays for most service work programs and organizations like the Red Cross and UNICEF. Without financial charity, there would be far less opportunities for service work volunteers.

I recommend giving at least 10% of your income to charity. When you do this and you begin to contribute to a cause far bigger than yourself, it expands your sense of purpose and impact in life. Suddenly, when you go out to earn money in the marketplace, it's no longer just yourself you're earning that money for. You're now earning that money for others as well.

The greater your purpose in life for earning money, the more money you will earn. Think beyond your own personal needs and wants. If you feel uncomfortable with this, then don't do it for others. Do it for yourself. It'll help you become more successful. And your success will have ripples that will make the world a better place.

INVESTING

Investing is another wonderful way to give back. Right now, you're probably reading this book on a Kindle or an iPad or some other electronic device. But without investors, that device or computer you're currently using wouldn't even exist! Like it or not, we live in a capitalist society, and some organizations and companies are so large that they need capital from investors to function and offer the best prices and value to customers.

By becoming an investor, you can engage in capitalism and help make the world a better place by investing in companies that help make the world a better place. Everyone benefits from a good investment in a good company.

MENTORING

Mentoring is another fantastic way to give back, and one of the most rewarding in my personal experience. Being a mentor to someone means you donate your time, knowledge, resources, skills, and connections in order to help someone else become more successful. Every time you help someone else take that next step forward in his or her life, it makes it easier for you to take your next step forward.

If you mentor others consistently and are honest with yourself, you'll probably find yourself giving advice to others that you haven't fully followed yourself. That's a good thing! Through mentoring, you can become conscious of your own shortcomings and opportunities for growth. And no, it's not being hypocritical when you do this. It's being honest. I highly recommend reading *Decisive: How to Make Better Choices in Life and Work* which explains this phenomenon of how we often make better choices for others than we do for ourselves. Becoming a mentor and teaching others is a great way to help yourself because you will become conscious of these shortcomings that you have been overlooking. It will also make a huge difference in the lives of the people you mentor.

Sharing Kindness

Sharing kindness with others is one of the most powerful and often underappreciated ways of giving back and making the world a better place. You never know how a simple thank you or smile given to another person can affect their life, and how the ripple effects of that one act of kindness can change the world.

If someone cuts you off in traffic, what is your reaction? Do you get angry or do you get grateful? If you find yourself getting angry, think of letting them in front of you as an act of kindness.

What if they're rushing a woman to the hospital to save her life? What if you saved her life by letting that car in front of you? What if she becomes the teacher for your child and her inspiration and guidance helps your child live a better, happier life? What if that guidance from the teacher saves your child's live?

When you start to see things this way, you realize that a simple act of kindness like letting someone in front of you in traffic is a blessing in disguise. Would you let a car in front of you in order to save your own child's life? Of course!

Our problem isn't that someone cut us off in traffic. Our problem is that we're often stingy. We have such a limited perspective of the world that we don't see all the blessings in disguise.

By being kind to others, sharing a smile or a few words of encouragement, we can change the world. This isn't some hokey, new-age philosophy. This is the truth. Little things matter. I guarantee that if sometimes you're a jerk when someone cuts you off in traffic, then sometimes you're a jerk to the people you love most.

Start practicing kindness right now with everyone you meet. You don't have to be perfect. Just practice getting better. Remember, little things make a big difference.

SPECIAL FACEBOOK GROUP

Come join our Facebook group just for readers like you who want to network, share ideas, collaborate, and connect with other like-minded people. In this group, we'll be sharing our successes, ideas, and strategies with each other so that we can all continue to achieve our goals and dreams in life.

Come join us here on Facebook:

facebook.com/groups/EntrepreneurSuccessGroup

Connect with Tom

Thank you so much for taking the time to read this book. I'm excited for you to start your path to creating the life of your dreams as a Kindle author.

If you have any questions of any kind, feel free to contact me directly at:

Tom@tckpublishing.com

You can follow me on Twitter:

@JuiceTom

And connect with me on Facebook:

on.fb.me/W8fA7B

You can check out my publishing blog for the latest updates:

www.TCKpublishing.com

I'm wishing you the best of health, happiness and success!

Here's to you!

Tom Corson-Knowles

ABOUT THE AUTHOR

TOM CORSON-KNOWLES is the #1 Amazon best-selling author of *The Kindle Publishing Bible* and *How To Make Money With Twitter*, among others. He lives in Kapaa, Hawaii. Tom loves educating and inspiring other entrepreneurs to succeed and live their dreams.

Learn more at:

Amazon.com/author/business

OTHER BOOKS BY TOM CORSON-KNOWLES

Secrets of the Six-Figure Author

Systemize, Automate, Delegate: How to Grow a Business While Traveling, on Vacation and Taking Time Off

The Kindle Publishing Bible: How To Sell More Kindle Ebooks On Amazon

The Kindle Writing Bible: How To Write a Bestselling Nonfiction Book From Start To Finish

The Kindle Formatting Bible: How To Format Your Ebook For Kindle Using Microsoft Word

The Amazon Analytics Bible: How To Use Analytics To Sell More Books

How To Make Money With Twitter

The Blog Business Book: How To Start A Blog And Turn It Into A Six Figure Online Business

101 Ways To Start A Business For Less Than $1,000

Facebook For Business Owners: Facebook Marketing For Fan Page Owners and Small Businesses

Rules of the Rich: 28 Proven Strategies for Creating a Healthy, Wealthy and Happy Life and Escaping the Rat Race Once and For All

How To Reduce Your Debt Overnight: A Simple System To Eliminate Credit Card And Consumer Debt

One Last Thing...

Thanks for reading! If you enjoyed this book or found it useful I'd be very grateful if you'd post a short review on Amazon. Your support really does make a difference and I read all the reviews personally so I can get your feedback and make this book even better.

Thanks again for your support!

Index

1

101 Ways To Start A Business For Less Than $1,000   43

A

action   iv, 5, 6, 11, 14, 15, 25, 26, 32
Albert Einstein   23
Amazon   14, 41, 43, 45
ants   v, vi
author   10, 39, 41

B

bad habits   30
Bangkok   19, 20
blaming   30
Blind optimism   vi
blindfold   11
blog   10, 39
both sides   vii, 16
business   iii, vi, xiii, xiv, xv, 5, 6, 20, 21, 24, 26, 27, 41
business plan   xiv, xv

C

challenge   iii, xi
challenging   iv, vi, x, 11, 18
charity   34
circumstances   viii, x
clear   iii, 9, 11, 14, 23
communication   1
conscious thinking   24, 25, 26
courses   xiv, 2, 10
creativity   22

D

dangerous   vi
Debt   43
defeat   3
difficulty   vii
disaster   v
dreams   iii, iv, v, vi, viii, x, xv, 5, 6, 7, 9, 11, 14, 15, 16, 25, 26, 30, 31, 37, 39, 41

E

eBay	14
embarrassment	17
emotional	v, vi, vii, 18
energy	8, 9, 34
entrepreneurs	xiv, xv, 41
excuse	vi, viii, xv
excuses	x, xiv, xv, 29, 32

F

Facebook	2, 37, 39, 43
Facebook For Business Owners	43
fighting	v
financial	iii, 1, 9, 34
Financial Crisis	v, vi
focus	4, 31
freedom	xiii

G

Gandhi	v
goals	iii, xv, 5, 6, 7, 8, 9, 10, 11, 12, 13, 14, 15, 16, 26, 30, 31, 32, 37
God	7
going with the flow	iv, v, 21
gossip	vi
grateful	x, xi, 18, 36, 45
Greek mythology	2
guarantees	iii, 3
guidance	vi, 26, 36

I

influential	viii
information age	2
investors	xiv, 20, 35

J

Jim Rohn	vii, 2
journal	x, 4, 5, 18, 21, 24

K

Kindle	ii, 35, 39, 41, 43
kindness	22, 36

L

law	ii, iii, 15, 20
love	vi, viii, 5, 10, 17, 18, 22, 34, 36

M

Man's Search for Meaning	viii
mentor	35
mistakes	24, 29, 31
money	iii, 1, 7, 8, 9, 12, 13, 14, 20, 25, 30, 34
Mother Theresa	v, 34

N

Napoleon Hill	19
negativity	vi
net worth	6, 8, 9, 12, 14
Nick Vujicic	viii

O

obstacle	v, vi, x
old habits	24
opportunities	vi, vii, x, 3, 30, 34, 35
opportunity	iv, vi, vii, x, xv, 33
Oprah Winfrey	viii
optimists	vi, vii

P

pessimists vi, vii
President Bush 20
President Obama 20
proactive 32
problem iv, vi, x, xi, 2, 10, 11, 24, 25, 26, 27, 33, 36
problem-solving 2
progress iv, 8, 9, 13, 14, 18, 26, 27, 30, 31
psychotherapy viii

Q

quitting 7, 31
Quiz Bowl 2, 3

R

Rajawongse 19, 20
realists vi
reality vi, vii, viii, x, 5
Red Cross 34
relationship 7, 17
research 2, 10, 14
resistance iv, vii, xiii, xiv, 3
risk vi, vii
Rules of the Rich 43

S

sacrifices 3
scared xiii, 30
Secrets of the Six-Figure Author 43
seminars 2
shortcuts iii, xiii, xiv, xv, 1, 12, 19, 23, 29, 32

Stephen Hawking viii
Steve Jobs v
stock market vi
study 1, 2, 4, 7, 8, 24
studying 1, 2, 3, 4, 6, 8, 27
stupor v
success iii, iv, xiii, xv, 2, 3, 8, 11, 15, 19, 23, 24, 26, 28, 30, 31, 33, 34, 39
successes 37
suit 20, 21
Systemize, Automate, Delegate 43

T

T. Harv Eker 29
talent 2, 4, 6
teachers 2, 26, 30
The Kindle Formatting Bible 43
The Kindle Publishing Bible 41, 43
The Kindle Writing Bible 43
The Secret iii
timing xv, 32
Twitter 39, 41, 43

U

UNICEF 34

V

value 21, 22, 35
Victor Frankl viii
visualize 15

W

Warren Buffett 8
wealth 7, 8
workshops 2